NORTH CAROLINA
STATE BOARD OF COMMUNITY
LIBRARIES
WAKE TECHNICAL COMMUNI

WAKE TECHNICAL COMMUNITY COLLEGE LIBRARY
9101 FAYETTEVILLE ROAD
RALEIGH, NORTH CAROLINA 27603

OUR SUN WILL RISE

821 Hou
Pegram, Amelia Blossom.
Our sun will rise :

OUR SUN WILL RISE
Poems for South Africa

Amelia Blossom House

Visual Responses By
Selma Waldman

Three Continents Press

Poetry ©1989 Amelia Blossom House
Artwork ©1989 Selma Waldman

An original by Three Continents Press
1636 Connecticut Avenue, N.W.
Washington, DC 20009

Library of Congress Cataloging-in-publication Data:

House, Amelia Blossom.
   Our sun will rise: poems for South Africa/Amelia Blossom House;
visual responses by Selma Waldman.
    p. cm.
   ISBN 0-89410-642-2 ISBN 0-89410-643-0 (pbk.)
   1. South Africa—Poetry. I. Waldman, Selma, 1938- .
II. Title.
PR369.3.H6909 1988
821—dc19   88-30779
                            CIP

All rights reserved. No part of this book
may be used or reproduced in any
manner whatsoever without written per-
mission from the publisher except for brief
quotations in reviews or articles.

*For my daughter, Melanie
and all the children of South Africa.*

Acknowledgments

Some of the poems in this collection have previously been published in *Fairleigh Dickinson Literary Review, The Gar, Staffrider, University of Louisville Minority Voices, Essence, Pacific Quarterly,* and *Genève Afrique.* The poems were put together with the encouragement of Dennis Brutus, Leon Driskell, Earbie Johnson, Hazel Yates, Stephanie Stokes-Oliver, and Lois Morris.

To begin at a beginning—
 If recollection serves, there is a short story for young people, a tale called, I think, "The Drum," by Chinua Achebe, and it begins more or less as follows:
 In the beginning of time, when the world was young....
 Then, of course, there is the early global belief, expressed as religious faith: the concept of divinity and creation—or as scientific theory—the notion that people are substantially homosapiens with the birth (the invention of) language!
 In the beginning was the Word (*Logos*), and the Word was....
 We may move next to the world-view of many Native American religions which regard as equally sacred and efficacious those rituals which are initiated, inaugurated and accompanied, energized and made continuous within a communal consciousness by means of drumming and dancing...
 And in the Far East, for Hinduism, it is true that: Lord Siva *danced*...
 So also, Dionysos-Bacchus and the Maenads are to be seen as animating forces—the tabor and the dithryambic rhythms of celebration are ultimately conducive as carriers of trance power, vital forces, and fire, etc.
 So that, finally we come to the conclusion along with Heraclitus that the universe is a life-giving fire in constant flux and in form-giving motion—dancing. Ms. House has it, in one of her poems, that:

  In the beginning was the dance
  And the dance goes on

It seems clear to me that it is this urge, this urgency, this pulse and electrifying beat, this breath of being and breadth of possible reference and allusion, that is the world of wonder and will which informs Amelia Blossom House's writing; hence the recurrent images of song, drum, dance, work—the cycle of birth, family, parenting, relationships, community, pain, healing, and renewal.

Ms. House's poetry lives in the community; she is from South Africa: the obscenities, evil, ugliness, the remedial blight that apartheid is, and that racism has been in many places, but most particularly in the Republic and the Union of South Africa, are realities that the poet as person, the cultural worker among the people must see, must say—as for instance in "Resettlement," "Dimbaza," and "Burials."

But in the compass of reality, and the pain and the pathos that they describe, these poems, and others like them, carry an awareness of the need to mobilize, to organize, to work for conscious change and for a social order that is life-enhancing, embracing mind, body and spirit in the total growth of the individual, encompassing individuality as self, with individuality inside the community and society, linking society with environment and life:

> We still dance
> past celebrations
> for the soul of the soil
> present celebrations
> for the fight of the soil
> future celebrations
> soul victory
> we still dance (WE STILL DANCE)

"I Will Still Sing," one of many poems of this nature in the present collection, relies on almost elementary lexical material to achieve a compilation of drama, philosophy, and music.

"Music!" Because one starts off by listening to a herald who is proudly self-aware, an individual who shouts with self-confidence, and yet is not self-centered. A community participates in the event, a ritual of joy and high purpose, a victory a happening that betokens success, regeneration, and song.

This poetry is such a flux and interpretation of ideas—cumulative multi-directional, and significant in the areas of history, culture, politics, *Weltanschauung* and life-style, and on levels of verbal organization as systems of sound, phrase, clause, sentence, and stanza, that their final "high sentence" precludes punctuation and visual stanzaic ordering. The poem is about a celebration; it is a chant, and praise, and satire, so it is structured in a single flow.

For how else does one signify the impetus and impact of synchronic totality, of the terrifying immediacy that life may generally have and that (particularly, but not uniquely) the South African black-white situation presents as confrontation and as a daily wearing and dismantling of fronts, of affronts, and confrontations...

The dynamic of the writing is such that systems of scoring its drama and music would clutter the page; instead, the simple words themselves become ringing symbols, resonant organs and systems that describe things, forces that grow, futures that must ensue, and of a history of yesterdays that are alive and must be recognized in their need for expiation.

"I Will Still Sing" is a poem that contracts and dilutes in inobtrusive tensions that reside in a thousand-and-one verbal crevices and crannies. But it is only one of many poems by Amelia Blossom House that achieves, almost completely, strain and stress under a simplicity and apparent limpidity to reach explosive truth, immediacy, life, and meaning. At their best, these qualities lie waiting in "At Dimbaza."

But rather than analyze that poem and its achievement, or examine the drive, power, and metaphysical vividness of "For South Africa," let me generalize and say of Ms. House's present poetic oeuvre, that its seeming effortlessness is a great daring and a startling presence, a complex, consummate truth, an experienced and experiential richness, an essential art and artistry.

It is of the essence of living and making. It is poetry. It is so aesthetically pleasing upon analysis, part relating to part, so replete with craftmanship and ease, that it seems to have generated itself and its own aesthetic.

I have read these poems to myself many a time, and also

read them often in public, inter alia on radio for PBS stations, on television for WVIZ (Cleveland) and WOSU (Columbus), and at public gatherings in Ohio and Pennsylvania. I have read them before small and large audiences of many tastes and backgrounds.

These poems speak to audiences.

I am glad to have read them, and am pleased to be able to write this "introduction" for poems that speak for themselves.

Cosmo Pieterse
Ohio University at Athens
Department of English

Table of Contents

Acknowledgments/vi
Introduction/viii

Poems

in the beginning/3
Birth of the Blues/4
Between/5
Sistersong/7
Awakening/9
Sunrise/11
Firecircle/13
Watchers/15
Tryst/16
Mr. White Discoverer/17-18
I Will Still Sing/21
Reflections/22
Survivial/23
Death by Birth/24
White Reply/25
Towards Abraham's Bosom/26
Resettlement/29
Red Accident/30
BOSS Birdwatching/31,33,35
Grandmother/37
Kinship/38
Soweto Jump-Rope/39
Truant/41
The Island/42
Dimbaza/43
At Dimbaza/47
Burials/49

Dirge/50
Freedom Fighting/51
Christmas '83/52
Hills/53
Exile/54
Return/55
Consolation/56
Chargers/57
Mother Leah/59
Hard Labour/60
For South Africa/63
Deliverance/64
Melanie/67
Sacrifice/69
We Still Dance/71

About the Author and Artist/72

Drawings

vii, 1, 2, 6, 8, 10, 12, 14, 19, 20, 27, 28, 32, 34, 36, 40, 44, 45, 46, 48, 58, 61, 62, 65, 66, 68, 70

in the beginning was the dance
and the dance goes on . . .

at your birth
you burst into the dance
to the lifelight of the circle

      and the dance goes on

we led you to the centre of the dance
we embraced you in marriage
as you learned to keep the cycle

      and the dance goes on

we marched to war
our feet dancing
to the pounding drum
for the fight of the soil

      and the dance . . .

you did not ask
to slow the dance or stop
as you slipped from the circle
in death

      the dance goes . . .

we remember you
in victory your spirit lingers
the lifelight glows in the centre
of the circle

AND . . . THE DANCE GOES ON . . .

Birth of the Blues

The beat was sure
Drums vibrating
Feet pounding
Hands clapping
The beat was steady
Hips rolling
Bodies circling
Colours sunrise
Setting
The beat was sure
Africa's pulse

galley-slaves rowing
rhythm
steady
drum rhythm
changing
the beat was flowing
lashing

The beat was steady
Flowing
Rhythm
Blue Water
Changing
Africa's pulse.

Between

the anvil and the hammer
dreams form
new worlds
shape perfection
between
the anvil and the hammer
dreams smoulder
passion
perfect harmony
new songs
waiting
metal on metal
dances suspended
between
dreams of perfection
anvil and hammer

Sistersong

Are you singing sister?
The song's the same.

Sing it softly
rocking
baby

Sing it swiftly
cooking
dinner

Sing it wildly
making
love

Sing it harshly
pounding
corn

Sing it loudly
washing
clothes

Are you singing sister?
The song's the same

You carry the melody
not
the licks
for you
the song
is always
the same.

Awakening

Between daylight and night
My Country
you wrap yourself in minksoftlight
Listen
as I play a tune for you
Listen
as I gently brush circles
on the swollen belly of the drum.
Flow with the brush
Lull to the beat.
Between nightlight and day
will be time enough
to leave the brush
to change the beat
My hands will pound the drum
Flesh on Flesh
Listen
to the scream

Sunrise

I'm tired
of watching
black clouds
roll across the sky
like Firestone tire advertisements
I raise my hands
beyond the clouds
the sun draws
my blood
to join its long fingers
to reach
through the darkness
Raise your hands
brothers and sisters
My blood
and yours
will make our
sun rise.

Firecircle

Out of your fiery womb
We danced
Circled reddust
        against the dawn
Our feet branded the soil
Now we arise
Through the pain of dispossession
Splashing our blood
        against the noonsun
Till we arrive
At the victors' circle
Arms raised, faces lifted
Soil reclaimed
To
Dance the red dust
        against the sunset.

Watchers

Silently
African woman
neck stretched
hips swaying
feet in mud
heavy loads
balanced
high
giraffelike
you see
above treetops
to visions of sweet fruit
each silently waiting
for the signal
when you join forces
African women
elephant stampede
through visions
to sweet fruit.

Tryst

tonight
soft and warm
i wait my turn
great Limpopo-fluid
        brownbody flow
you'll come
dip in my warm waters
let the night air
echo   echo
your singing thighs
roll in the heat of my mud
        surround you
stop daybreak
tomorrow
day-clean
the music stops
        the air stills
i carry my waters to the sea.

Mr. White Discoverer

to cover your shame
you tied
my sunkissed breasts
tied
imprisoned
my swinging breasts
now
when
earthlight
merges into
my black body
then
phantom lover
you
come
unleash
my breasts
white feet
dancing
out of step
wrap
trap
my legs
im
moral
ity
acts
sucks
my milk
But
Mr. Whitey
no blood
fevers

through my
untuned body
No more
no more
tonight's
last
moonkisses
my breasts
tomorrow
my beads
tune
to sunkissed
swinging breasts

Mr. White Discoverer
cover
your shame.

I Will Still Sing

It is my celebration
I will drum my drum
I will sing my song
I will dance my dance
I do not need your anemic hands
brought together in pale applause
I do not need your
"You are such musical people"
toothy smile
It is my celebration
You wonder what I have to celebrate
What does the drum tell me
If you must speculate
Watch Out
One day as you throw your head back
As you gather your hearty laughter
I will change my dance
I will still sing
The drum will scream
Celebration.

Reflections

You said
Fair equals beauty
And Snow White
Heard
"Who is the fairest?"
Mirrorless
I believed
My image in the muddy river
Wasn't fair
Fair equals beauty
Reflections
Speak true
As moonlight to sunlight
I believed

But

In your mirror
My unmuddied reflection
Was beautiful

Black is Beautiful

And Snow White
need not ask
"Who is the fairest?"

Survival

I can be happy
without joy
laugh
with no laughter
smile
with my teeth
Because
You say
I am happy

Yes, Sir, Yes, Ma'am
Come easy too

I can dance
without rhythm
sing
with no song
celebrate
without reason
Because
You say
I have musical rhythms

Yes, Sir, Yes, Ma'am
Come easy too

I cannot live
without freedom
dream
with no vision
die without peace

No, Sir, No, Ma'am

You do not say.

Death by Birth

CAPE TOWN. 21.50 15 AUG. 1967.
"Daddy in accident. Died this evening."
CAPE TOWN. 9.45 p.m. 13 NOV. 1900.
Born
      accident
colour black
died this evening
classified
      non-person
destiny
      non-existence
group areas
job reservation
immorality act
education
      black
      accident
"Daddy died this evening."

White Reply

You are born in your coffin
Black Man
You have no skin
Black ebony - wood
Do not pretend to be alive
Do not cry out
Do not strike your coffin
Black Man
We will not answer
We bury our dead
Stay in your coffin
Die in your coffin
Rot in your coffin
Black Man

Towards Abraham's Bosom

White cloth spread
Table Mountain
welcomes
All of no colour
to a banquet
While
on the sandy Cape Flats
Icy winds whip tattered clothes
cut through cracks
Empty bellies rumble
Frost-split feet shuffle
Huddled in plastic body bags
discarded
black bodies
wait
While
No blacks feast
We wait
for the crumbs.

Resettlement

red blanket
spread on
brown earth
i travelled
on cloud ships
across sky oceans
sunburnt eyes
watched
over my spread brown earth
Then (it was **DECLARED**)*
no longer
could i
lie on
red spread blanket
i sat
crouched
unable
to travel
on cloud ships
i watched
bulldozers invasion
my blanket
corners crosstied
i was hoisted
deposited
on Limehill.

*Area DECLARED no longer for Blacks under Group Areas Act.

Red Accident

Off the Cape
Indian
meets
Atlantic
dolphins play
submarine
frolics
seaweed slides
off the Cape
warm
Indian Ocean
pulling
yellow sand
twisting
cold Atlantic
tugging
yellow sand
dolphins play
submarine
silver blues
off
the Cape
sub
marine
white light
nu
clear
explosion
seaweed
slides
twisting
dolphins

Boss Birdwatching*

Sing Canary
Fly
and Die

We set our trap wide
for the Bikobird
He soared
the eaglespan
admired
by the little birds
They could learn
to fly
like the Bikobird
high wing-spread soar
But
we watched
caught him in the swoop

Sing Canary Sing

Clip his wings
reduce his size
pluck his feathers
a naked bird will
sing

Sing Canary
Fly
and Die

*(Boss: Bureau of State Security,S.A.)

An eagle no more
The Bikobird
dead.

Sparrowlike Timol moved
quietly
meeting all
the little birds
telling all
the news
of nesting freedom

We gently
lured the sparrow
but
he wouldn't learn to sing

Canary Sing
Fly
Die

The Imam
in beautiful robes
hovering
over his people
a hummingbird
sweetness transmitted
gentleness
swiftness
admired
by the other birds
they could learn
to
drink the sweetness

Our captive
hummingbird
had no voice

Sing Canary Sing

Pluck his bright feathers
stop the flapping
Cut his beak
canary size

Sing Canary
Fly
and Die

Sing Canaries Sing.

Grandmother

The hanging
was at dawn
my grandmother
Madame Defarge-like
reserved her seat
her wrinkled arms
like old knitting
folded
my grandmother
came to watch
the freedom-fighters'
hanging
but
reserved her seat
for the next hanging . . .
of
the hangman.

Kinship

Shall I call you
My Brother
Because
You turn your palm up in greeting
Wear an embroidered dashiki
Your black face glistens
Under a mean Afro?

I shall own you
My Brother
Because
You have danced in the circle
To the beat of the drum
You have shared my dreams
Worked boldly
To make the dreams reality.

Soweto Jump-Rope

did you hear my mama cry
did you hear my mama cry

they dragged her out of bed at dawn
we clung screaming to her skirts
they took her to a bad bad cell
now we're left at home alone

did you hear my papa cry
did you hear my papa cry

woken by their midnight raid
kicked and hit him for their fun
they threw him in the waiting van
when he'll be back we do not know

did you hear my sister cry
did you hear my brother cry.

Truant

He stayed from school today
bad Billy bad
boys of eight
don't protest
South Africa's laws
bad bad Billy
don't call names
don't throw
sticks and stones
break policemen's bones
bad Billy bad
policemen beat with sticks
throw gas
bullets tearing
in the back
dead Billy dead

                (for Cape Town Sept. '76)

The Island

in the cold harsh Atlantic
merciless waves lash
no escape reminders
to rock breaking inmates

in the cold black Atlantic
the island keepers
welcome free seagulls squawking
no escape reminders
to be back broken inmates.

Dimbaza

If all my tears
can stay the last
grave at Dimbaza
I will weep
But I have seen
our fathers' tears
harden with blood
which could not prevent
the last
grave at Dimbaza
I cannot weep.

At Dimbaza

three by two by two
                times ten
today
   tomorrow
      tomorrow
         times ten
no time
     for six feet deep
             but I have no tears
today
   tomorrow
just two feet down
the new-opened earth
lies in wait
         no time
for six feet deep
three by two by two
        times ten
today
   today
      tomorrow
no time
     for me to cry
     for six feet deep
but
   when I see
the last grave at Dimbaza
              today
                  tomorrow
I will cry

Burials

dear God
i didn't kill the butterfly
i only buried it
in the foilwrapped matchbox
because
i wanted it still to be pretty
for you
i sang one hymn
cried a little
i tend the grave
i found the dead sparrow
i buried it
in redcrepewrapped shoebox
"All things bright and beautiful"
i sang again
but
dear God
it's not because i loved burials
i don't need
five or ten daily
i don't know
what to sing
those children of Dimbaza had no time
to be
bright and beautiful
i have run out of hymns
I cannot cry all day.

Dirge

D r u m
for the dance
of new children of Africa
Drummm
Children
born
as mothers squat
on city sidewalks
Children
growing thin
their highlife
nightclub trashcans
D r u m
for the dance

Drummm
for the song
of new children of Africa
D r u m
Children
born as mothers labour
in country
reddust
Children growing thin
feeding on lizards
death's
messengers
Drummm
for the song
mmm

Freedom Fighting

Was it yesterday I left my native land?
I'd come to taste of freedom with the exile band.
Freedom to live
Freedom to learn
Freedom to speak

Was it yesterday I left my native land?
I'd come to taste of fighting with the exile band.
Fighting for life
Fighting for truth
Fighting for speech.

Was it yesterday I left my native land?
I've not tasted of freedom fighting with the exile band.
Learning to live
Living to speak
Speaking for freedom.

Christmas '83

Shall I sing of tinsel ivy holly
mistletoe
hung high
Or hum Silent Night through sleighrides?
Is Christmas angels shepherds
and a new-born child?
Or nothing more than a Ho-Ho-Ho?
the shepherds heard
                  Fear Not
The baby brought good news
                  Peace on Earth
except to Iran, Iraq, Beirut, Grenada
and sundry other places.
The message came
                  Goodwill to all men
a message not heard
by the KKK or the Boere* in Pretoria
So I'll sing the song
of Ho-Ho-Ho
of eggnog and good cheer
of chesnut-stuffed turkeys
ivy holly tinsel
mistletoe
hung high

*Boere (boors) Afrikaans plural of Boer.

Hills

on this cold january
in the hills of kentucky
snowcovered bluegrass
send laughing children
speeding the slopes
and one january
i will return
ignore "Whites Only" signs
to roll down open sand dunes of Hout Bay
climb the hot yellow hills
to suck the brown juice of the sourfigs.

Exile

Exile
is not leaving
capetown
or coming to
kentucky
or being in london
paris or rome
but knowing
there is no easy going
back.

Return

I've left my heart
in many countries
but
I have my home
in only one
I yearn to return
claim my place
in
South Africa's sun.

Consolation

huddled in layered cloth
by the flickering fire
i wait in exile
where in january
the river icebound
imprisons the python
who cannot arch
his colours across the sky
draped in flowing green chiffon
out of exile
one balmy breezy january
into a jacaranda scented evening
i will return
to pavostrut*
under the southern cross.

*pavo—'peacock' constellation in southern sky.

Chargers

The deathcarriers
rode the white horses
to my shores
tossed destruction
on my shores
I send
you
my sons
to ride the ocean
tame the white horses
learn their pale secrets
return for the
Charge.

           Mother Leah weary of
Lipservice lament for South Africa
Empty-eyed children waiting
Abandoned through live-in dreams
Hopes shattered on Soweto streets

                Leah, Mother of Africa
                weary of weariness

                of the fight for the soil
                of raising voices of defiance
                with the soul of sadwa
                weary of movement against rebirth*

MOTHER LEAH

teaching new songs and praise
new hopes and fights
for family-embraced children
in free Soweto sunshine.

(for Leah Tutu.)

*sadwa: South African Domestic Workers Association

Hard Labour

When we are condemned for planting seeds
of freedom
Pain
we must endure
And
when you bulldoze our planted fields
to destroy our freedom harvest
Pain
we must endure
But
when our deep rooted crops escape your
freedom crushing
And we tend them with back breaking labour
Pain
we
will
endure

For South Africa

Like a woman gone
beyond her time
        My Country
you amble on
with a heavy burden
        pressing low
you amble on
we can no longer
wait for nature's course
we must deliver
You
  With
    Force.

Deliverance

Bear   down
My Mother Country
Push
You who have carried the seeds
full term
Bear   down
Push
Only you can give birth
to our freedom
Only you can feel the full
ripe weight
Bear   down
We will stand by you
We must relieve your pain
Bear   down   Bear   down
Push.

Melanie

Child of darkness
          born
into the light
you must keep
          burning
to help in the
          struggle
to make
blackness
          right.

Sacrifice

At your birth, my daughter
I heard you cry
a lamb unblemished
my new offering
to the world.

At your birth, my daughter
I heard your cry
for my pain
And your births
to come.

We Still Dance

today
yesterday
tomorrow
through and beyond time
we still dance
red dust
black mud
ochre sand
we still dance
birth
marriage
victory
death
we still dance
ankle rings
bracelets
feet drumming
soil
we still dance
yesterdays celebrations
for the soul
of the soil
todays celebrations
for the fight
of the soil
tomorrows
soul victory
we still dance.

Amelia Blossom House was born in Wynberg, Cape Town, South Africa. She received a B.A. from the University of Cape Town. After teaching in South Africa for seven years she went to London. While teaching in London she studied drama at the Guildhall School of Music and Drama. She acted in London on stage, television, radio and film. She has lived in Kentucky since 1972. She received an M.A. degree from the University of Louisville in 1977. At present she is teaching in the Fort Knox Community Schools System and part-time at the University of Louisville. Dennis Brutus, the South African poet is her present subject of study. She has had short stories, poems and critical essays published in many countries. She has read her poems in the United States, Canada, Norway, and England. She prefers to 'perform' her poetry with percussion.

Selma Waldman received her B.F.A. from the University of Texas. She completed her studies in Berlin at the Hochscule für Bildende Künste under a Fulbright Grant in 1961. Between 1963 and 1967 she completed a series of life-sized drawings on the Holocaust, more than 25 of which are now in the collection of the Jüdische Abteilung of the Berlin Museum. Since 1965 much of her work has been conceived for human rights causes. Her graphics for Liberation Movement Publications documenting African struggles for self-determination, have received international attention. Waldman lives in Seattle, Washington, where she has taught drawing since 1966 in art and alternative schools, and in Adult Education at the University of Washington.

ISBN 0-89410-642-2
ISBN 0-89410-643-0 (pbk.)

821 Hou
Pegram, Amelia Blossom.
Our sun will rise :